NEEFYISM
FROM ALLSTAR TO LIFE

NEEFY MOFFETT

© 2023 by Neefy Moffett
Neefyism
From All-star to Life

All rights reserved solely by the author. The author guarantees all contents are original and do not infringe upon the legal rights of any other person or work. No part of this book may be reproduced in any form without the permission of the author.

Scriptures marked NKJV are taken from the NEW KING JAMES VERSION (NKJV): Scripture taken from the NEW KING JAMES VERSION®. Copyright© 1982 by Thomas Nelson, Inc. Used by permission. All rights reserved.

Unless otherwise noted, all scripture is taken from the NEW INTERNATIONAL VERSION (NIV): Scripture taken from THE HOLY BIBLE, NEW INTERNATIONAL VERSION ®. Copyright© 1973, 1978, 1984, 2011 by Biblica, Inc.TM. Used by permission of Zondervan

ISBN-13: 978-1-737-27686-9 Paperback
979-8-218-22873-6 Hardcover

LCCN: 2023911931

Broken To Mended Publishing

Melbourne, Florida

Typeset by Michelle Cline

NEEFYISM

FROM ALLSTAR TO LIFE

NEEFY MOFFETT

ENDORSEMENTS

"When I think about Coach Moffet, I think of him as more than just a coach. He has been a mentor, a father figure, counselor, and a friend. When you first meet Moffet you will ask yourself, who is this crazy, loud person and how can we get him to be quiet? But just from that first encounter you will get to know the kind person he is. He is a loving, caring, man of God, a man of many traits, a family man, and a comedian. These are all traits that come to mind when trying to describe him. All in all, he is a character. He has made a huge impact on my life. He has taught me many life lessons that have helped me transition in the stages of my life. He has been there for me when my life was at my lowest. He motivates and encourages me to continue to dream big and accomplish all of the goals that I have set for myself. Most importantly, he has taught me it's okay to be myself. Being my authentic self, no matter what! That includes loving myself with the good and the bad, while embracing being different. He took me in like I was his own son, and I will forever be grateful for everything he has done for me. If I could describe Moffet with one word, I would say it's spontaneous. You will never know what he will do at any given moment."

David Exum
Mentee

"Neefy has always had a big impact in my life since the day we met. I remember the first time I met him... I walked out of Ms. Dooley's classroom, and he asked me, "why aren't you playing football." I told him my grades were the only thing that was holding me back. He had me meet with him afterwards to help me with credit recovery. We talked about school, life & positive ways to make money. I grew to love Neefy like my older brother. From the first day we met, he always treated me like family. I respect him so much because I don't have the best family besides my immediate family. They all treat me the same! It went from helping me with school and graduating high school to being invited to dinner, playing with the girls, and watching our sons play together, and building a forever relationship. He's a person I could always count on... and I'm not talking about money situations but someone I could call for advice. He does play a big role in my life and I'm thankful I found someone as solid as he is. He's shown more love and loyalty to me in a few months/years than my own flesh and blood have my whole life. They don't make people like that anymore. He would never steer me wrong, and he's always been completely honest with me.

It's crazy, sometimes I sit back and reminisce while we're at his house playing. I don't have anyone in my family that I could sit over at their house and play the game, eat dinner, and feel 100% comfortable. Besides my grandfather, Dad, and my wife, I really don't have anyone else. He makes up for everything I didn't have growing up. We can relate to so many things in life because we've been through and are still going through similar things. It makes my eyes water writing this because I

Endorsements

really couldn't count on anyone growing up. I've had my back against the wall so many times in my life with no one to help me... nobody to talk to and nobody could ever understand me. My father was in prison so I couldn't call him for help. I couldn't ask my mom for advice on questions about growing up being a man and I didn't want to put that type of stress on my grandfather. So I had to grow up faster than the average person. When I met Neefy he was everything I needed... guidance, a role model, last but not least, a genuine person!"

Clint Bryant
Mentee

DEDICATION

This book is dedicated to my family. Evelyn I love you baby, you inspire me more than words can ever explain. Erynn, Gabi, Eva, and Gavyn, I can't expect you to live your dreams and not be the example of doing it first. This is the first stop in our legacy, the bar is set high for you guys. Let's not forget that the bar is always doing our best, to live our dreams and believe in ourselves. Mama, thank you! Watching your life showed me that I can have what I want for mine. I remember eating at McDonald's by force not by choice, but you always believed that wouldn't be the outcome for us, so you changed your life and showed us that our situations are only temporary, but visions and purpose are forever.

This book is also dedicated to you Geno, we talked about writing a book since we were teenagers, and I finally did it bro. I hate that it is you leaving this earth for me to do it. To my family, I love y'all and want to be the example to live out your dreams no matter how wild they sound. To my mother who instilled that situations are temporary, but my salvation is forever.

TABLE OF CONTENTS

Introduction		xiii
Chapter One	Keep your eye on the Ball	1
Chapter Two	Love and Marriage	9
Chapter Three	Navigating Rock Bottom	17
Chapter Four	Knowledge is Power	27
Chapter Five	Starting with the End In Mind	31
Chapter Six	Counseling	39
Chapter Seven	The Truth Set Me Free	45
Chapter Eight	HARP	49
Chapter Nine	Managing Emotions	73
Epilogue		85

INTRODUCTION

First, I want to thank you for purchasing my book. I have thought about creating this book for some time but for many reasons it was not until this present day that it is possible. I believe that God's timing is perfect, and I am finally able to share these insights with all of you. I am a firm believer that we can learn from other people's wisdom and experiences and with this in mind, I am putting this content out there for you to benefit from it. After working with children of various ages and in different capacities, I noticed the strong need these children and teens have for guidance and knowledge in order for them to navigate their everyday lives. They don't need to be told what to do. In fact, that is part of the problem. When you teach people what to think instead of how to think you create more problems than you solve. For example, growing up I was always told about Jesus and how I should see Him as the savior of my sins. I thought about this for a long time, and it shaped my life. It made me think I was bad and needed to be saved. I felt I wasn't deserving of things because I was so unclean and needed to be washed by the blood of Jesus. When I read the Word for myself I learned that Jesus said whoever believes in Him will do the work he does and also do greater works than Him because he was going to the Father, and we were staying here.

I was so perplexed at this that it sent me to research so much more. I found out that many things I was taught were not in the bible but rather what someone else taught them and it was just passed down. When I learned how to think from Philippians 4:8 *"Finally, brethren, whatsoever things are true, whatsoever things are honest, whatsoever things are just, whatsoever things are pure, whatsoever things are lovely, whatsoever things are of good report; if there be any virtue, and if there be any praise, think on these things,"* my self-esteem levels have been astronomically high. What I offer in these following pages are principles that can be applied to a variety of life's situations. Keep in mind that another principle is the truth shall set you free. When you take a deep dive and find these truths, you will never be the same. These principles will allow you to give them the ability to make decisions on their own that will lead them on a path to success. As a child grows older a parent should be able to exercise less control over their choices and instead offer guidance and assistance as they work through the decision-making process. Afterall, our children are adults in development.

What I share are principles regarding the core concepts that I find need the most attention in these young adult's lives. Understanding the importance of decisions made regarding marital relationships, future parenting, knowing how to recover after setbacks, and understanding the importance of education just to name a few areas I discuss in this book. As a teacher, a coach, and a parent, my experience in these different roles and environments has given me a perspective others don't have and that points to troubling trends I see in today's young adults. The lack of purpose, many of them unable to make decisions independently, difficulty to create life goals, and a constant need for guidance and direction.

On one occasion I was on the way home from a track meet, and I had three of my athletes with me. I listened to them talk about how they were depressed and felt fortunate to have track as an outlet. They struggled with self-esteem issues; they were not happy with how they looked or how they felt. The conversation turned to the frustration they felt over the constant battle of trying to perfect. If you gain too much weight, you are fat, or you lose too much weight, you are a "crackhead". Hitting the social 'sweet spot' of being just right was a burden every one of them carried. Hearing this I was heart-broken, proud, and purposeful all at the same time. It broke my heart to hear kids going through all these feelings about a simple task needed to live, 'eating'. I felt proud because at the time I was a father of three girls and my daughters didn't share those types of thoughts or feelings. I felt validated and I knew I was doing a good job as a parent. My daughters have the liberty of sharing their thoughts, goals and dreams with me and they were never like this. That's when I realized I was more than a mere coach, I was a father figure, a mentor, and a molder of young adults. I grew very compassionate and driven to do my best every day because even on my worst days I was someone's best hope. I had to research and develop new skills to avoid having a bad day again. My granddaddy Marvin used to say, every day is a good day that he's on this side. I never understood it until he died. Now I have the opportunity to live that out for myself first but for others. It's like I realized I was blessed to be a blessing.

It also brought to focus how we are losing our young ladies early. Too much of the conversation was focused on problems with boys and their desire to be free of those issues and not enough about their future and goals. Their thoughts and minds are being clouded with problems that should be left for adult relationships. I was humbled by this experience and know that God has put me in this exact place to be able to hear these conversations and speak on them. I took them out to eat that night at Chick-fil-a because I was still feeling heavy hearted. It blew my mind that some had never been there before, and they poured their hearts out to me. One even said, *"I'm over here telling my life story. I never talk to anyone."*

This is exactly the end result when you provide a safe place for them in which they can be vulnerable, without feeling judged or fear they will be treated differently because of their current situations. There are too many voices, too much noise capturing their attention, and someone has to provide an outlet, a safe place for them to feel the liberty of sharing while feeling safe.

The reason I chose the topics that I did for the book is because they reflect what I wish I would have known at a younger age and what I feel the younger generation is lacking today. I am purposely providing you with insight and conversational topics so that you can discuss them with your children, friends, family members, or any youth groups that you have access to.

Introduction

I can still recall the frustration I felt when I was younger, and I didn't get drafted to the NFL. When I went to FSU, the defensive coordinator, Mickey Andrews asked me what my goal was in coming to FSU. I told him I wanted to be the highest drafted player in FSU history, at the time it was number 3. My goal was to be picked 1 or 2 in the NFL draft. I felt like I had worked my whole life for it, and I even put myself into a position to get it. I played sports year round; I was determined to make it. When I was 13 years old in the 8th grade I remember striving to leg press 10 plates on each side. Calculating the weight now shows how a little ridiculous I was. That was 1,025 pounds I was trying to push as a 13 year old. I worked really hard to maintain a 3.0 grade average in high school while being one of the top athletes in the nation. I played basketball to maintain footwork and conditioning in the offseason, as well as ran track to get faster and more explosive. I did 5 events, 100m, 200m, 4x100m relay, shot put and either discus or high jump. This was year round all throughout high school to put myself in position to be drafted. It wasn't just a dream, I deserved it! I felt I earned it, and it still didn't happen. I tried keeping my eyes on the prize, which I thought was to have enough money as an athlete so that when it came time to be a mega pastor, people knew I wasn't going into ministry for the money. I missed out on several years of my life. I missed out on the college experience, meaning socializing, having fun, being irresponsible, staying up all night studying, going to parties. I also missed out on opportunities to connect with people through vulnerabilities and experiences because of being focused on the wrong thing. That's why it's very important to keep those eyes on the prize. I had to go through several hardships and trials to be where I am today, but I can say now, it was all worth it. Everything that we live and go through becomes part of our testimony and through those very same experiences, we are able to inspire and help other people.

This book is an example of keeping the end in mind, I always saw myself as a speaker, and this book is the first step to creating my own reality. I had to see myself as who I am today before I could ever do this. I am not perfect, nor have I learned it all. I acknowledge I am still a work in progress in many areas, and it's the reason why I want to shed some light on these topics. These principles can be taught to children and young adults. The message can be adjusted to be age appropriate, using examples and situations they currently face as children or young adults. The sky's the limit when you are the author of your story.

Teaching children over time how to become independent is more successful because it gives them experience and it gives the parents the opportunities to observe and provide guidance and any needed correction. As parents we will never be able to prepare our children for every situation that will arise, but by teaching them how to think instead of what to think we can give them the tools they need to be able to successfully overcome obstacles they may encounter.

Proverbs 22:6 says: *"Direct your children onto the right path, and when they are older, they will not leave it."* When we read this in the Scriptures, it is not just referring only to the word of God in itself, but in all matters. The guidance and insight we provide to them today will show fruits in the future, and this includes everyday decisions and principles.

Tell them that when they get to that fork in the road, to read and apply these principles in their lives so that unlike me, they won't be fighting an uphill battle in quicksand. Know that God is the same before, now and will be, and if He did it for me He can surely do it for all.

CHAPTER ONE
CREATING YOUR OWN REALITY

All things are created twice. First, they are created in your mind and second it becomes a physical reality. You must know what you want before you ever take any physical action. It does not make sense to get in your car and start driving without a destination in mind. But, knowing is only the first part. You must determine where you want to go in life and what it will take to get you there. Then you have to act accordingly. For example, it is one thing to say you want to become a professional athlete. However, if you skip practice, go out the night before games or do things that are counterintuitive to your goals, then that goal will not be met. You must show the same amount of commitment to your goals physically as you do mentally and vice versa. A plan is great and necessary to have but if you don't take the necessary steps then that plan is just an idea.

I'm sure you know someone who always talks about wanting to start a business, travel the world, even write a book—the list can go on and on. They talk about it almost every time you see them, but they never do it. They think about it. They sometimes even started the first step towards the first process but never got past that point. Be sure not to clutter your mind and give your time to goals that are nothing more than daydreams. Save that time and energy for those things you intend to put the effort towards carrying out. When you hear others say, *"I can't believe I have gotten to this point in my life,"* my bet is if they are honest with themselves and take a hard look at their actions leading up to that point, they can see exactly why they are in their current situation. When your actions are not aligned with the desires and goals you have set in your mind, the result will be an outcome that you did not desire or 'plan' to happen.

For instance, I had always planned to be a husband. I knew I wanted to get married and have a family. In my mind, I know I can be hard to deal with. I see things in their most simplistic form and find things are either black or white. So, I decided that it would be during my years in college that I would marry the woman who would be able to tolerate me during these years. However, I didn't just want to be married; I wanted a happy marriage. This is very important to point out because one thing is to be married and another is to be happily married. I learned that a good first step towards achieving your goals is to look around and find others who have already done it. Search for those who already have the knowledge. Watch them, ask them questions, and then imitate that behavior that made them successful. That is exactly what I did. I went and found mentors, men, that were living in those types of relationships and studied what they did. I needed to understand the work behind what it took to be a part of a happy, healthy marriage. I began to mentally prepare myself for what I envisioned before ever physically trying to manifest that reality. During this personal process I came across these five steps that helped me in my journey and can serve as a starting point for you.

THESE FIVE STEPS WILL HELP YOU START THE VISUALIZATION PROCESS:

Get Clear on what you want. Before you start visualizing, it's important to be clear about what it is you're looking to achieve. In business, profit, growth, recognition, a great new product, and happy employees are great places to start. Identify those things you wish to achieve in any given area of your life whether it be in education, sports, spiritual, financial, family or any other given area first. Have a clear goal and be confident to explain it with a few words as an elevator pitch.

Keep it general. While athletes get very specific about the landing they want to stick to, or the race they want to run, life and business goals can be less specific. For example, I prefer visualizing profit and growth over a specific revenue number. This will help you to continue growing, expanding, and achieving different goals without placing limits.

Use images. Having images to look at really helps your mind latch onto what it is you're trying to achieve. Maybe it's a photo of the perfect weekend cottage you'd like to have one day, or the image of an MBA from a great school. Having a visual reminder will help keep you focused.

Visualize often. Glance at your vision board multiple times a week, if not daily. Make it part of your morning routine. Glancing at your vision board or closing your eyes for three minutes and visualizing your goals is a great, positive way to start the day—or end it.

Don't trade it in for hard work. Visualization won't replace working effectively. Like Olympians, you still need to put in hours to achieve results. But visualization can act as subconscious programming, bringing opportunities to your attention that you may miss otherwise. For me, visualization is an indispensable daily technique for achieving success. It hasn't won me any Olympic gold medals, but it helped me drive great results and bounce back from tough times. Not bad for a scrapbook.

With all of this said, ask yourself the following questions: What are you giving your energy to? What are you trying to accomplish with the life that was given to you? You have to know the answers to these questions. You can't get what you want if you don't know what you want. Once that is established, start acting as if you already have what that is. This will change your thought process, your perspective, and your behavior. Dig deep; try this on something small and build from there until you trust the process.

Don't just settle into your current reality; alter it. In order to fully understand how to be intentional with creating your own reality, you must first know what reality means. If we do a search on the internet, you will probably come across a definition like the one below:

Reality:
The quality of being real

- A real event, entity, or state of affairs

- The totality of real things and events
- Something that is neither derivative nor dependent but exists necessarily

The truth of what you wish to achieve is not limited to your current reality. Remember that things exist first in your mind and then when you take action it becomes a tangible reality. It all begins with a mindset.

Michael Phelps said of his technique, *"One of the things that has been good for me I think, besides training, has been my sort of mental preparation."*

Olympic medalist Katie Ledecky has said: *"I have my goals and I visualize things to help me achieve those goals ... I know what my stroke should feel like at different parts of the race, and I can just kind of picture that in my mind." (Inc. August 2016)*

REFLECTION

1. If you had 100% success in anything that you would do, what would you do?

_____

_____

_____

2. Is anyone doing what you envisioned for yourself, if so follow their steps, if not you get to create exactly how you want it done.

_____

_____

_____

3. How would your actions change if you got the things you wanted in question one?

_____

_____

_____

4. Create a vision board for yourself, be clear and as bold as you can be.

_____

_____

_____

Chapter One

This could be overwhelming and a bit scary, these are normal feelings when it comes to this. Write down how you are feeling, the more you read it the less strong the feelings will be.

_____

_____

_____

_____

_____

_____

_____

_____

_____

_____

_____

_____

_____

_____

_____

NEEFYISM

CHAPTER TWO
LOVE AND MARRIAGE

All my life I have been told that when a man finds a wife, he finds a good thing. I feel so deceived about that. It's a comment that it's sickening. It has been majorly manipulated over time and used to be an asset for some and a burden for others. When picking a spouse or partner it is paramount that you go in with a plan. Understanding that you are making a connection for life with this person. It should be careful and thoughtful with the end goal in mind.

Too many times we look at the beauty of a person and we miss the essence of who they really are. When it comes time to begin a relationship with a partner, never compromise your goals or dreams. Rather put your head down and run as fast as you can and go as hard as you can towards your goals and dreams, when you come up for air, look to your left and right and whoever is there with you, that's the partner for you. evaluate who they are in every environment. Look at their parents, the family structure they come from, their customs, their beliefs, and their future goals. Make sure it's aligned to what you want for your life because if not, those will be the biggest and most recurring fights that you will have. I recommend you go into a relationship with a spouse based on how you see your life, how you want it to be and how you want it to be maintained for your lifestyle. Know that there is no perfect relationship and that together you will have to pivot constantly, but when you and your spouse walk towards the same type of lifestyle, the end result is a lot better. Compatibility is a better word for it, make sure y'all interests are aligned and it's effortless to spend time together. If you both enjoy nature, being in nature is a way for y'all to enjoy your personal desires and spend time with one another without it causing strain on either of you.

I have found that those are the relationships that last and are able to maintain the same quality of life together. Long lasting friendships are built on common ground. Too many times we sacrifice who we are to get the girl/guy that we want, and both end up miserable, overweight, unhappy, and unfulfilled. You have to know that someone was created just for you, everything you could ever imagine in a man or woman has been constructed and waiting on you to come discover it. With that type of belief there is no need to settle for anything. It's not a matter of if, but rather when this will happen. That keeps you optimistic, open minded, and joyful while enjoying your journey of life.

While deciding who your spouse will be, make sure you first know what you want. For example I created a silhouette of the woman that I want to be with, but I also identified what type of husband I would like to be. Mine were shaped by my favorite people in the bible because I was unaware of any living examples of what I wanted. With modern technology you can find whatever you are looking for on the interweb and model their characteristics for yourself. Once that's established, believe that you deserve what you want. Then start acting as if you have already received the partner of your dreams, rather than going out and trying to create what you want physically and give thanks to the Most High because it is already done, you now just have to prepare yourself for the things that you want. When you master that, your spouse will be right there with you. Like the old proverb says, if you want to go fast, go alone. But if you want to go far, get a partner.

You will come to understand this proverb better when you are in a relationship with your spouse and life hits you with unexpected blows. This is when you will discover if the person that walks by your side has a similar mindset to yours or can be compatible with the ways you deal with stress and unexpected turnouts. This is tough and became very real to me when I heard a report about my son having development delays. Initially I was thinking of staying calm because she was already worked up and there was no point for us both to get worked up. My wife was hysterically crying, very sad, I hadn't heard her like that since her mother's funeral. We were on the phone, and I was actually at a track meet. I had to make an immediate decision at that moment. Do I let the kids down who believe in me and were depending on seeing my face at their events because their parents were working, or do I stay behind and console my wife? At the time, we had been at odds emotionally speaking and had been talking very little to each other. We were pulling up to the track meet with several students in the truck jamming to some of the latest tunes. I got them out of the car and settled, and then I began to pray and speak life into my wife, reassuring her that our lives are in God's hands and since we are submitted to him, he's obligated to do what he said he would do. This brought comfort to her heart. Scenarios like these are going to happen in your life, so be patient to choose a partner because it's a lifelong decision. Marriage is a beautiful thing when done with the right person. I was aware that I wanted a happy, long-term marriage, so I took my time in choosing my partner.

Make sure to apply this theory in every aspect of your life. You should only want what works best for you, for the things that you have planned for your life and your future goals. Strive to have the best because when tough times come around, this is when you will know if you chose right. I know that it has been said many times, but choosing a spouse only based on their physical appearance does not guarantee a good match. Don't idealize your partner. You are looking for a person that is going to pray harder for you than they do for themselves. You are not auditioning for a movie role; this is the person you are willing to grow old with.

Now learning how to deal with rock bottom will be very important because we are aware that there are mountains and valleys. I want to be transparent in telling you that the good always outweighs the bad, but the bad is still present. Learning how to navigate that before it comes puts you in a position to be more susceptible to success.

REFLECTION

1. With the life you have created, what type of partner will best support your lifestyle?

   _____

   _____

   _____

2. Now you have the qualities of your spouse, what exterior will be on this person? What physical characteristics would you like your spouse to have?

   _____

   _____

   _____

3. What are 5 things you would like to enjoy with your spouse?

   _____

   _____

   _____

Understanding that there is a chance you only get 80% of what you listed previously, are you willing to go without one of the things you've listed? Write out how you would feel each characteristic was missing. You will be writing 5 separate situations down.

Chapter Two

CHAPTER THREE
NAVIGATING ROCK BOTTOM

My rock bottoms have moved and changed throughout my life. As a matter of fact, just being born I had to fight for my life because my mother had viral meningitis. I thought my world was over when I was in the fifth grade. I had been going to the same school since kindergarten and was very well known. We had recently moved about a mile away from our previous house and this move put me in the district for another elementary school, but I was able to remain where I currently was.

My mother allowed me to remain there because I had been going there for so long. One day, late in the school year, we were at P.E playing funny ball, a mix between softball ball and kickball. I was the only student who had a different set of rules from everyone. I couldn't hit one away with the ball because I was too strong and fast enough to run them down and tag them. Well on this day, my schoolmate Kate was taunting after I got her out. I have had enough of it. She hit a grounder down the third base line, I scooped it up and from the third base line caught her dead in her thigh on her left leg in full stride running to first base. You would have thought I shot her with an M-16 the way she was yelling and carrying on after I got her out. My teacher bought the performance and immediately got upset with me and let me out of the game. Well, that day I had something to say, and I asked him about her part in the taunting and trash talking. He wasn't trying to hear it, so then I got mad and started raising my voice. He sent me to the office for my part, and when my mother came, she said that this was the last straw. She said I was moving schools. I thought my life was over, mind you I'm eleven years old leaving all the friends I grew up with to go to this foreign school where I knew no one. At eleven that was my first rock bottom experience, but I surely learned it would be my last.

Fast forward to 8th grade, I was coming off a basketball season in which I had to quit mid-season because I received two C's on my report card. I had busted my butt to be ready for track season, trying to defend my records in the shot put and 100-yard dash. I was extremely eager to get back competing again. With a lot of hard work, my grades were back to straight A's, and I was excited. After leading the team in the warmup stretching, I was pulled out by the dean of students and brought into the office. They said I was being suspended for ten days pending expulsion for my role in what was at the time, "typical teenage boy behavior".

Growing up we played a game named "Letter B" and if you said any word that started with a 'B,' a group of guys would just punch you until you said, "letter B". This one student, let's call him Joey, said a slur of words that started with a 'B' while walking home from the bus stop and so we began pounding him. He started to yell: "No! Wait! Timeout!" That didn't stop

Chapter Three

us one bit because the code word for us to stop was "letter b". Well in the middle of the beating he yelled, "I'll give you all dollars tomorrow if you stop". We agreed, because in the year 2000, one dollar meant something at the store. Well, the next day at the bus stop he hurried to get on the bus and sat in the front. We waited until we got to school and caught him while transitioning to the cafeteria for breakfast. He said he didn't have the money and that he would bring it the next day. A teacher walked up to us, and we dispersed like any off task middle schoolers would do. That moment led to me being picked up from track practice and being expelled from school for threat and intimidation, tampering with a witness and extortion. As a kid I thought I was going to jail after working so hard to make it back on the team. Then this happened.

Let's fast forward again now to freshman year in high school. By this time, I was 6'2" and 185 pounds of muscle. My older brother had been on the varsity football team, and we had been playing football together my whole life, so I thought I would be too. Well after the brief seven game freshman season when we went 6-1, I was primed to make the move to varsity. I had been practicing with varsity and on scout team defense and even tackled our senior college bound tailback a couple of times. I was finally getting my groove back until I got the news, *"No freshman will be dressing for any of our playoff games."* I was disappointed because I felt and knew I was truly capable of making a significant impact on the team. Just so happened that year in the playoffs, the injury bug hit us in the final four at my position and we ended up losing the game because we couldn't contain the quarterback, breaking a 24-game winning streak that year.

Now onto basketball season, my best friend Robbie had made the varsity basketball team as a freshman and I was excited to play alongside my buddy but to my dismay, I went to freshman basketball. With no disrespect intended, I felt I was on a completely different level to the rest of those freshmen. First game freshman year tip-off, I tipped the ball to my cousin Jamel. He took two dribbles and threw me an alley oop. I don't recall hanging on the rim, but I got a technical foul and that was my first and last game playing freshman. As a freshman I dominated the Junior varsity ranks averaging an easy twenty points, and twenty rebounds a game. I finally earned my spot-on varsity that year when we went to the playoffs. I was a post player, and I couldn't score that many points, but I was a fearless and tenacious rebounder. We traveled to St. Thomas High School in Fort Lauderdale, Florida where we faced one of the top teams in the state. I didn't expect much playing time but to my surprise our other post player had four fouls in the first quarter. I was extremely excited to get my number called but it never happened. My coach put an undersized guard on one of the top big men of the state and we went on to lose the game and get knocked out of the playoffs. I couldn't understand why my coach didn't call for me and on the three-hour bus ride home I really questioned myself and felt how I could get out of this hole. I felt let down with no options to have made that experience any different. I just had to trust it was all a part of the big picture called life!

The final fast forward as a new college grad, having a wife and an infant. We were living in Fort Lauderdale with my in-laws for the time being. I went and got my teacher's certification and

Chapter Three

through a relationship I built in college, I now had a coaching and teaching opportunity in Jefferson County, Florida. This was about six hours driving from Fort Lauderdale. I packed up my young family, and we moved to Tallahassee, Florida with the last of our savings. My wife was in school at Florida Agricultural and Mechanical University at the time, so I was willing to take the twenty-five-minute commute to work daily. I rocked the interview and already had my family move to Tallahassee. Then, the Friday before I started my new job I got a call from my coach friend, I could hear something was wrong in his voice. He told me that state laws stated that they must go with the most experienced teacher if the school is below average and on the last day of the open application someone else applied, knocking me out of the position. I felt like I let my family down and I was a failure. Here I am, a new husband with a 4 month old baby and a wife who is in college. I'm the man and I need to provide for my family and my only means of providing for them just slipped through my fingertips. I felt like a failure and that I wasn't adequate enough to be a husband. I wasn't a provider, and I wasn't deserving of life, let alone being a husband and father. Luckily, I still had a coaching stipend, however that only paid $1800, and I couldn't support my family off that. I was back at square one, but now I still had to share the news with my wife. She didn't take the news well, she felt it was more pressure added on her. She was overwhelmed, frustrated and angry. It was a rough season, but again I was able to overcome it and the same way I had worked hard to achieve every other goal, I had to do the same to support my family. I reached out to one of my former teammates who was the head of security at one of the local bars in Tallahassee. I figured that by working at night and watching my kid by day, I could save on childcare. I could make sure I cooked all the meals and kept the house clean. I did all that while still searching for jobs during the day.

Rock bottoms come in every shape and form of life. There is a floor to every level of life whether you are in the penthouse or the basement. We must learn this lesson early and keep moving. Situations are temporary unless you stay there mentally and physically to make it permanent. Rock bottoms are going to be there, use them as steppingstones to continue to move forward in life. Now we need to learn how to deal with rock bottom because we are aware that there are mountains and valleys. As I said in the last chapter, learning how to navigate before it comes puts you in position to be more susceptible for success. The bottom will end, it's not permanent until you quit. Looking back over my life with the perspective I have now, I realized every struggling situation in my life was a steppingstone for the life I am living now. Whether it was me losing a job before I got it, feeling like I was being held back in Arena Football, or seeing fluid on my son's brain, it was all part of a higher purpose. They all were critical pieces to the puzzle that shaped my thoughts and actions to this day to have this amazing outlook on life and the boldness to share my story.

Rock Bottoms can be part of life, but what you do with your failures or negative outcomes and how you react to them will determine if these failures can be part of your success. Let's mention a more famous example. For the sports fan, Derek Jeter is one of the most successful athletes of the modern era. While known for his intangibles, he was a sure handed fielder at the tough Shortstop position. Would you believe me if I told you he made fifty six errors in one season at the beginning of his minor league career? The Yankee organization sent him to a camp where they identified his pattern of failures and replaced it with one of success. If you prepare for adversity, when it comes it won't surprise you. Developing mental resilience is an important part of achieving success in life.

REFLECTION

1. What is your greatest fear?

_____

_____

_____

2. Plan on your greatest fear happening, what are you going to do next?

_____

_____

_____

Once you thought about it, you were able to plan on how to deal with it, it no longer made you fearful but rather a planner. Discuss the thoughts and feelings you have experienced while working through the plan. Write them down, when you are experiencing a rock bottom, come back to it to help you.

___

Chapter Three

CHAPTER FOUR
KNOWLEDGE IS POWER

I see how this one may be in left field; however I am an educator. I have a B.A. in political science with a minor in child development as well as a master's in educational leadership. I have seen a lot of students and while parents are thinking they are being educated, they are really being babysat.

Education is the knowledge and development resulting from the process of being educated, this is not necessarily what's happening in classrooms, and I think parents should understand. Education inspires you to be a free thinker and provokes action. If your children aren't constantly asking questions and showing interest in what they are doing, they aren't being educated, but rather indoctrinated. Our kids need an education that forces them to use their critical thinking skills and to move forward in their life. A lot of times we were told as kids *"Do what I say, not what I do, meaning don't follow the example that I am putting in front of you, but rather follow what I say,"* or just because I don't do it like that, it doesn't mean we can't do it. If the light within a child is dimmed or shut out early in life for whatever reason, we are left with zombies; a lifeless character that goes through the motions without feeling or thoughts. We have to break the generational cycles of ignorance and lack of basic life skills to survive alone, which takes them out of the competition of life. Our kids need to have the ability to hear something and recreate it in their minds. They need the ability to think critically in simple or complex situations. Our kids need to be able to take information and apply it practically. What do I mean by that? Good question, let me explain. On everything that we buy there are instructions for assembly. If the instructions say, remove the tab and screw in the handle, our kids don't need not to ask, what are we screwing it with? How do we screw that? They just need to look at the picture, get the right screwdriver twist and turn to get their work done.

Too many times we are not educating our kids but rather bullying them down. Our brains atrophy as our muscles. When we make all the decisions for a child and never allow them to think, grow, and make mistakes, their brains start to atrophy while still being developed. Now that sounds horrible and no parent wants that for their child, yet it continues to happen. Why is that you may ask? Well, when you take a thinking opportunity away from a child, subconsciously they believe they're not smart enough to complete the task. Generally, no parent just goes and calls their kids stupid, but by not letting them handle some things on their own, essentially that's exactly what they are doing.

Let's say you ask a child what is six multiplied by five times, and you see their brain working but you blurt out the answer before you give them the chance to answer; you just stopped the development of that child and discouraged them from doing that again. The result of this are kids that are not thinking because they do not believe they can. This transfers into the classroom, and in an environment that is meant to be competitive, the kids now make horrible efforts and have poor mental participation. This is how we combat this situation; we give our kids tasks and time to complete the mental process in order to get the minds properly developing. This sets up our kids to make informed decisions later as adults. When they have the capacity to apply what they know, this turns information into knowledge; knowledge that they created by applying critical thinking skills. Keep in mind that our kids are adults in training, approach raising them in that manner.

REFLECTION

1. What is something that inspires you to know more about it?

_____

_____

_____

2. What are some things you can do to learn more about what you answered in question 1?

_____

_____

_____

CHAPTER FIVE
STARTING WITH THE END IN MIND

GETTING TO COLLEGE

At the time I attended college, Andre Wadsworth was the highest Florida State Seminole drafted into the NFL. He was the number two pick of the Arizona Cardinals in the 1998 draft. It was one of my goals, the only one I fell short of meeting, that I had set for myself during my college years. I wanted to be the highest drafted player in FSU history. Even when I was younger, I always had goals set for myself. I wasn't just aimlessly roaming through life waiting for something to happen to me. I made sure that the choices I was making on a daily basis were ones that would ultimately get me to my goals.

I have come across too many young adults who have no clue as to what they want to do when they graduate. The time to prepare for adulthood is not when you become an adult. People need to begin developing a mindset that enables them to envision where they want to be early on in life, so that they can create a plan that will help them reach those goals.

Don't let the work discourage you from setting high goals for yourself. Instead of focusing on the end goal and how far away it seems, break down the steps needed to reach the goal. Although it may take time to accomplish your goal, this will help you see the progress being completed along the way. Celebrate achieving small and major milestones along the way to keep you motivated.

STARTING WITH THE END IN MIND

Starting with the end in mind, what does that really mean and how does it look? Well let's look at this. When I went to high school, I had a plan: get my college paid for, and my mother had a rule. If you don't go to college you are going to the military. We didn't have the funds to pay for college and I knew that. At graduation I wanted a full scholarship to college. As a freshman walking into high school, I had this mindset. What it did was guide my thoughts and ultimately my actions. I ended up finishing my high school credits as a junior, so my entire senior year was simple to say the least. Office aide classes, weightlifting, gym, and a bunch of electives that made it a breeze to the finish line, because I did what I needed to do at the beginning to get the desired end result.

The end can be interpreted as death, but in this case it is not. It's the end of the task that is currently at hand. When I went to college, I had plans to get drafted higher than Andre Wadsworth, find a wife, graduate, and have a lot of fun in the process. Looking back, I see I did all of those except get drafted higher than Andre, who at the time was the highest drafter Florida State Seminole ever. He went number two overall in the NFL draft.

Too many times, we don't look at the end before we start a task. My favorite book tells me that before I take a job, I have to consider the work it will take to complete the job. This principle is very important because it puts a premium on finishing. Too many times we start tasks and do not finish them, hurting people in the process because of our lack of consideration.

REVERSE ENGINEERING

Another tool that I have discovered along the way that has helped me with these concepts I have shared is reverse engineering. I have found that if I start off by visioning a successfully completed goal and imagining what was required to get me there it can help me identify what I need to do.

The four keys to reverse engineering for success are:

- Determine the most basic level of the goal.
- Ensure that you are committed.
- Identify as many steps as possible that are required to reach the goal.
- Take action!

I have found that if I start off by visioning a successfully completed goal and imagining what was required to get me there it can help me identify what I need to do.

In order to get started, you begin from the most basic stripped-down version of whatever your goal is: work from home, move to Central America, become copywriter, a pirate, anything …and break it down to the basic components that are required for you to succeed. Make sure to stay on track, celebrate the small steps conquered towards your end goal and do not stop moving. Stay on track and when you reach your goal, dare to start new ones.

As coaches we are always telling kids to keep their eye on the ball. This applies to life also, not just in the game. To be successful in life you need to be able to focus on what is important and tune out the distractions. When you go up to bat you must have a plan. When you go into high school, you should have a plan. It doesn't have to be exact but know the direction you want to go. Knowing you want to go to college after is not enough.

- What college do you want to attend?
- What does it cost?
- How will I pay for it?
- What are the admissions requirements?

These same questions should be asked by those beginning college.

- What employers do I want to work for? If so, what do I know about them, their company values, the way they operate and possible opportunities within them.
- How can I build my resume?
- Do I want to work for myself, and if so, what do I need to do to make that happen?
- Am I building positive relationships that will help me advance in life?

Chapter Five

Having goals not only on the field, in school, and professionally are beneficial, but also in our relationships. You are the people you surround yourself with. People will either lift you up or bring you down. Not everyone should have full access to you. Save that for those who share your vision, work ethic, and values. I will say this and it's a hard reality but very necessary, everyone isn't meant to go to the finish line with you. Let's look at Moses. He didn't make it to the promised land, but we still hold Moses in high regards. His role was to get them from Egypt to the promised land but to never be in there, that was for Joshua. Relationships, no matter how important they are, are on a cycle. Some cycles are like mangroves, like the ones we have here in Florida. They never wither or fall because they are connected to the water source. To go a step farther, they filter the water, retain what is good or the fresh water and expel the salt, that's why if you like the back of their leaves it's salty. Some are like other trees where the leaves fall off once a year and they grow back. That's fine too, but you just have to be aware of the season in which you want to depend on them. When you find like-minded people that build on your commonalities instead of differences, value them and keep them close.

REFLECTION

1. What do you know about your great great grandfather/mother?

　

　

　

2. What would you like the — on your tombstone to represent?

　

　

　

Write a letter to your love ones and date it 50 years. What is it that you want them to know about you? Tell them what you are doing today to effect their lives 50 years from now. Spare no detail and leave no stone unturned.

Chapter Five

CHAPTER SIX
COUNSELING

This has been a struggle for me to understand the concept of this word. I have been to anger management counseling, marriage counseling, as well as individual counseling. When I was younger, I used to think of it as sitting in a big chair and talking about my problems, while they sit and tell you what's wrong with you and you leave feeling better. With this level of thinking my first bout of anger management counseling was unsuccessful. I was in college at the time, and I wasn't angry, I just felt like everybody had it wrong about me and it frustrated me. I was so misunderstood to the point where I began to be standoffish and started shutting down. My counselor, who's name I forgot, was really frustrating to me as well. She kept asking me about my childhood and who hurt me and why I was so angry. Her trying to make me angry was making me angry. and It seemed like that was what she was trying to do; to create a narrative of the angry black man. Let's just say, this didn't work. I didn't go back to counseling again until I was there now for a divorce. It never went through; however this time counseling was different.

Dr. Atkinson made it about me and how my outlook on things really curves my reality. In the counseling the word that most bothered me was vulnerable. I learned so much about vulnerability that it completely changed my life. I thought being vulnerable was to sit and be a helpless duck and let people attack and do what they want to you. It was a very weak word in my mind and I'm no weak person, so weakness was no option. Upon researching, I found that vulnerabilities are the tentacles in which you connect with others. I learned that being vulnerable made me relatable to people and it really opened up my connections with people.

I could remember telling my story of the time I wanted to commit suicide. I went to go kill myself, but I remembered reading TD Jakes' book when Deion Sanders drove off an overpass in rush hour traffic while in Dallas at the pinnacle of his career and had a failed attempt. In September 2010, I was ready to end it all. My oldest daughter was one and almost two at the time and I just had enough. Nothing in my life was going right. I came off of a year in the AFL (Arena Football League) where I felt like I was great, I rushed the passer like no other and felt like I was being held back from moving up to the Canadian League. I had a job as a dependency case manager for a firm I won't name in Tallahassee. Before I left to go to Jacksonville, I had gotten the job back after the season, so I thought. A week before my return after confirmation, seventeen high ranking officials got fired and my name got lost in the mix. My wife who was young at the time (twenty-one) had not been practicing empathy and the pressure had boiled over and I was done. I kissed my daughter goodbye, I told my wife to make sure that my daughter knew that I loved her, I walked out to the car, called my Bishop, Bishop Jacqueline D.

Gordon, and told her I was done. She prayed but at that time I wasn't trying to hear it. I was out praying to God about the right spot to go, so that I could finally meet him.

As I'm writing this it sounds crazy to pray to God about committing suicide, but I did. Writing this now has me thinking back to why I even called her. God had his hand on my life back then as well. This is how Deion inspired me, as I was riding through hilly Tallahassee, to Florida and I prayed to God and asked him to tell me the right turn to make because I didn't want to be like Deion and mess this up, *"Lord I want to be sent directly to you."* Thank God he didn't answer that prayer and I am here to tell this story. This is part of my story and because I had enough sense to listen, I am telling you this today. When I told that story on my podcast *"Real Garage Talk"* on YouTube it started gaining views and I found myself having random conversations with people about keeping their head up and that tough times don't last, tough people do.

I was such an emotionless robot when it came to many things. I said things like, *"I feel with my hands,"* meaning how I feel about a situation that is not acknowledged, it's gone, get done. My feelings don't matter because I'm still gone, so why even bring them up. She challenged me to look deeper within myself and to see why I was like that. This is when marriage counseling became individual counseling. I had tremendous strides from that experience, and it really opened up my mind to what counseling is supposed to be.

The clinical definition of counseling is- *"A relationship in which a professional or trained individual attempts to help another, so as to understand and solve his or her difficulties in psychosocial adjustment; counselors may also advise, opine and instruct in order to direct another's judgment or conduct."*

This was not what I originally wanted or used it as. I looked to my bible in the book of Proverbs where it says: *"Where there is no counsel, the people fall; But in the multitude of counselors there is safety."* That challenged my thinking of the situation, and turned it from a negative aspect, to a positive one. What I understood is to respect the wisdom elders have since they always have your best interest in mind. When you try to do everything alone and keep everything inside you will fail. I learned to share my situations and vulnerabilities with people in order to connect with them and help them see they are not alone. Now, I have a team of people around me who go through similar things, and I learned that talking about them, not complaining, is a way that we stay connected, grounded and mentally sound. We don't need someone to tell us how to fix our problems or help us with them, but rather listen, let us get it out and make room for the solution to present itself. I understand now that a counselor's job isn't to fix you, but rather give you tools for you to "fix" yourself.

REFLECTION

1. What is something that you have on the inside that you haven't shared with anyone but have been dying to get it out?

_____

_____

_____

2. How does it feel to finally get that off your chest after all these years?

_____

_____

_____

Take a deep breath and remind yourself that you have this. That moment isn't going to control your life, rather, you will take back control of your life. Remember that we are in this together and that your ascension is based on how much unnecessary weight you drop. This next part is the most important part of this book. Write down everything you don't want to carry with you on your journey of being the best version of yourself.

_____

_____

_____

NEEFYISM

CHAPTER SEVEN
THE TRUTH SET ME FREE

BEING HONEST WITH MYSELF

So, for a very long time I held anger in my heart and thought that I was wrongfully prosecuted and black ball, although some of those things might be true, the reality of the situation is that I wasn't in the NFL because of my own thoughts. It wasn't that I wasn't good enough because I was. It wasn't that I wasn't a good fit because I was. In my prayer God revealed to me why I didn't go to the NFL, and it was the most humbling experience of my life. Now let me give you the backstory, I loved Reggie White growing up, a believer that played football, I also loved TD Jakes. I wanted to mix the two, but what was loudest in my ears was that mega preachers are taking money from the church. That consumed my thoughts. My mother also told me football was a way to an end, not the end all be all. That's when I developed the thought process of going to the NFL to get the money and then becoming a mega pastor and although that's not a bad idea, people like Miles McPherson have done it. I was doing it only to get the money so that people aren't saying I'm exploiting God's people.

God showed me that he isn't in the business of blessing for that purpose. It was a huge revelation for me, by my own words and thoughts it cost me my dream because of the intention. If I wanted to be in the NFL, I could have done it, being a mega pastor is still an option but the reason behind the why matters. I share this with you because I want to encourage you to ask yourself why you want the things that you want. God is fully capable of providing the desires of your heart, but we have to understand that: *"But the LORD said to Samuel, do not consider his appearance or his height, for I have rejected him. The LORD does not look at the things people look at. People look at the outward appearance, but the LORD looks at the heart."* as said in 1 Samuel 16:7. If our heart isn't right in our asking, we won't get it. So, make sure you are honest and genuine in your desires. As I am putting on the finishing touches of this book before it goes to editing, I can honestly say I feel the best I have ever felt in my life. I feel a huge burden released and I can have true joy, and not just temporary happiness. A lot of times people are told that life comes in waves, and you aren't supposed to get too high on the highs or too low on the lows. I had that way of thinking until I came to the understanding that whom the Son sets free is truly free indeed, John 8:36. I never knew why there was a need to emphasize the indeed until now. Freedom can be perceived in so many ways that the need to be free indeed was necessary. That indeed shows that not only do I look free on my exterior, but I am free on my interior. Paul said I can do all things through Christ that strengthens me, (Phil 4:13), but he wrote that from a Roman prison waiting for execution. Seems like he wasn't free physically, but he was because he understood he had eternal life (John 3:16). When you can be honest, genuine, and sincere there is nothing that can take you out of that moment and you see that the truth is setting you free from everything, including your own thoughts and agreements.

REFLECTION

1. Is there something that you want to clear up about any part of your life?

___

___

___

2. That was major, forgive yourself for holding on for that for so long.

___

___

___

CHAPTER EIGHT
H.A.R.P

Harp is an acronym I came up with, with the help of a friend. It is what I have learned to live by. It gives me the most peace of mind dealing with students, parents, friendships, and mostly relationships. It was designed with what women want in mind but after further review, it is actually what people need. In my opinion, this is the key to world peace and although I've never wanted to win a Nobel peace award, this may be the key to world peace. This formula has been shared with a few people in my circle, however, now I'm ready to share it with the world. I will break down each letter in the acronym and then show you practical applications on how to use it in your everyday life. Whether you're in a relationship, marriage, broken family, or just want to be better with people, this is for you.

HONESTY

Honest—free of deceit and untruthfulness; sincere.

Let's unpack this before we dive headfirst into this one. To be honest means to not deceive others, trying to make them believe something that isn't. The sincere part is kindness, so when you are honest, it's done with kindness or it's not honesty at all, it's cruelty. Cruelty is callous indifference to or pleasure in causing pain and suffering. So now that we have established a baseline for honesty let's look a little closer.

We first must be honest with ourselves to even be honest with anyone else. I had to look at my life and say, I am not going to the NFL! That is gone, what can I do next? That's when I remembered what my mother told me when I was growing up, football is a way to an end but it's not the end. It's a game not your life, you are way more than football so don't get caught up in a dream. She told me this before I ever started playing organized football. In my time of need I had to look within myself and truly be honest with myself. I'm never going to try to hurt myself with my words or do anything that I feel is not in my best interest and that is the foundation of human interaction. The golden rule tells us to love others like we love ourselves, but I am here to challenge that thinking. I believe we have had it wrong the whole time. I think the golden rule was lost in translation and that it should be to love yourself so you can love others. When we truly love ourselves our love for others spills over and the by-product for others is a genuine, sincere love for humanity. Once we have that level of honesty we move forward.

When being honest with a person, you are interacting with people in how they show up, not what they are showing. One must be in tune with themselves to hear and understand that. A lot of people are just paying attention to what people are saying. In communication, 70% is nonverbal, so if we are only listening to the words, we are missing the vast majority of what is really being communicated. That's why after careful deliberation and sound tutelage, I've adopted the "listen to PEOPLE but don't listen to people" theory.

A lot of people are taught to keep it real, but they never understand what they truly mean. I battled a long time with the truth and being honest. I thought for the longest they were the same and they aren't. True- in accordance with fact or reality; accurate or exact. Truth is based on reality and exactness, whereas honesty is based on sincerity. They are cousins not twins. Once I let that go and understood that those things aren't synonymous it helped me out tremendously. Direct honesty is a reflection of oneself and the level in which you use it is a direct reflection of how honest you are with yourself.

When I felt like I was insufficient and incapable of being in the NFL, I had to truly be honest with myself. I needed to really look within and ask myself the hardest question of why. When I realized that Reggie White influenced my game as a defensive end and minister, I really wanted to use my platform to spread the gospel; or what I had known the gospel to be. When I was younger, I loved church but hated how people would talk about it, God, and their experience.

I had a real-life experience when I was 16 years old coming home from homecoming. I was with my boy Tadd. We were out past curfew heading to my nanny's house (grandmother), to try to out-think my mother and extend my curfew. That night when we were at his friend's house, I fell asleep, and he had been drinking. I made the decision to drive because I thought it was the safest route. When I got in the car, I put on my seat belt and went to adjust my seat and the chair broke. It was stuck in a down position at 180 degree angle. I took off my seat belt and proceeded on the 6 mile drive to my nanny's house. I remember talking to my girlfriend at the time who I had lied to, and she was very upset with me. I truly believe the arguing kept me up that long. After getting to the light at Malabar Rd and Emerson drive, I turned left and that was the last thing I remember before hearing a rumbling sound. I woke up and saw a concrete mailbox and I made a sharp left turn. I remember the first loud crash and then I blacked out. I don't know how long I was under or anything else until I felt a kick getting me out of the car.

We were upside down and I was in the back seat. When my friend got out I climbed out and followed him. He took off and ran. When I chased him down our conversation helped me understand why he ran. He was currently on probation and would have been locked up for violation. I wasn't sure how much time had elapsed, but by the time I got back to the truck, which was upside down on the driver's side, people had been gathering and the police were pulling up. I called my cousin Eric, and with no hesitation he was up there in record time. The police said there were eyewitnesses, and I wasn't the only person in the car. I completely denied all of it and I ended up getting a ticket for reckless driving. I almost got off, but one officer said I needed to call my mother because my cousin couldn't be my guardian. By this time it was 4:00am, and when my mother got there she remained quiet. She picked me up and as we were driving off the police waved us down and gave me the tickets. I maintained my story of being alone, however my mother knew I wasn't because it wasn't my car. I went home and went to sleep and during that time she received a call from my friend's mother, and she filled her in on the details of the night. It was her car.

I tell that story to say that my views on God have never wavered and it always hurts me when people would talk so badly about church. I wanted to go to the NFL to gain the money only to be a mega pastor. So when I didn't go to the NFL I had to really be honest with myself. This is the first time I am publicly telling that story. Some of my closest friends don't have the details of what I shared. That's the type of self-honesty that allows me to deal with others honestly. It's completely out of love. My story is a bit extreme to some but a reality for me. I'll stand it against anyone's and that's why I go so hard and believe in the matters that I do. I walked out of the accident with literally just a scratch on my eyelid. That night I realized God has a plan for me and no matter what I think the plan for my life is, that night is a reminder to always consult with God.

The practical application of honesty in people should be first being honest with yourself, then allowing people, time, and space to be themselves. My best friend, Kita, always reminds me to watch people's motives and don't interfere; they will get it when they get it. When you deal with people honestly, you will remain calm and understanding. You won't get swayed from left to right because of their actions because you understand it has nothing to do with you at all. This is the first step to complete cooperation in the HARP process to achieve total cooperation with people.

HONESTY WORKSHOP

After you read the section above on the honesty portion of the H.A.R.P concept, take some time to answer the following questions. Make sure that you answer as honestly as you can. The answers are meant to help you to identify areas that you might need to work on and having this workbook section can provide you with good insight.

- What relationship do you think you need to mend the most?

- Being honest with yourself, what role did you play in the downfall of this relationship?

- Forgive yourself for what you said in question 2. The healing process will always begin with forgiveness and many times forgiving ourselves is the hardest step. This step will always provoke a breakthrough in your life.

Identify something you can do to continue moving forward in your progress. Take your power back! Your vulnerability will be your superpower, get everything out that could fuel your freedom.

Chapter Eight

> # ACCEPTANCE
>
> **Acceptance** -the action or process of being received as adequate or suitable, typically to be admitted into a group

Acceptance starts from within. I made a list of all my strong points as well as my weak points. I'm not going to lie, my strengths were easy to identify, but my weaknesses were hard to admit and even to write down. It took a true sense of vulnerability to even write it down let alone admit these things. This is true courage because I'm about to share with you what I found out about myself. I had big lofty dreams but had no action behind them. I always knew I was going to be rich, but I never had a plan. I was a big dreamer and I spoke about my dreams, but I wasn't much of a doer. I was a fake, and as hard as it is to read, it's even harder to say about myself. My boy Toddrick used to tell me all the time I was full of crap, not in those words though. In my mind, everything was just going to fall into place. That's when I learned that God doesn't work like that. He told Joshua in the book of Joshua, *"I have already blessed where your feet will walk, so be strong and courageous."* (Joshua 1:3). I was shown that every prayer in the bible was answered no matter what they prayed for. Jesus said, give us this day our daily bread in the lord's prayer and that prayer was answered. Paul asked for the thorn to be removed and God answered, *"My grace is sufficient"*. Agur in the bible asked God for two things, give him riches or poverty, and keep liars away from him, and God answered. Jabez asked for his territory to be enlarged while God kept his hand on him so that no evil could harm him, and God answered that prayer. That led me to believe that I was doing something wrong because I didn't have the things I dreamed for. My biggest issue was I didn't pray about it first and secondly I didn't pray to get it. Now when you pray you have to understand that God answers it immediately. It's done the moment you pray for it, however most prayers aren't answered because you don't prepare for what we are praying for. That's why the bible says in the book of James that faith without works is dead. Pay close attention to the word "works" not work. It's not a merit based system, so we don't work for our grace and love from God.

Works is a mental thing. We must believe that what we have prayed for is already on the way and we are preparing for it. For example, I have 3 daughters and a son. There is a 7 year difference between my youngest daughter and my son. This matters because my boy Gooch (Jeremy Johnson) used to always tell me that the world isn't ready for another Neefy Moffett, so no matter how many kids I have they will all be girls. My next two children after that were girls, so I shut down and was content with having 3 girls and I totally embraced the "girl dad" thing. Remember when I told you my wife left me several times? Well this last time before my son was born I was in CVS talking to my brother Dontaie about our new living arrangements. I was leaving my house and I told him that after this break up I was going to have twin sons, Gavyn, and Enzo. Today my son's name is Gavyn Enzo Moffett, or GEM because he is precious to me. That's an example of works at work. It's all in your head. You must believe no matter how it looks from the outside. That's faith, according to Hebrews.

"Faith is the substance of things hoped for and the evidence of things not seen." (Heb 11:3 NKJV). If we can see it, it's not faith and we know from Hebrews 11 that it is impossible to please God without faith. All in all, Toddrick was right, I was full of crap because I wasn't doing three things and I didn't accept myself. Now there is a whole level of boldness and faith I live by because I have acceptance. Whether it is in my faith in God, accepting myself for who I am, or accepting people for who they are, acceptance is layer. Once you peel back one level there is another until you get the ultimate form of acceptance. So if you are on the first level of acceptance please don't get discouraged. What I told you about acceptance for me was a 15 year journey. I'm sharing my experience with you so that you can see where I am today and see that I have made mistakes before. But my mistakes don't identify who I am. Rather they helped mold me into who I am today. They were grinders in the shining process so that I can stand boldly before you today in this form.

When we start to accept others, we no longer try to change them, and we can appreciate them for who they are. We never know what people have going on in their life and shouldn't judge them by how they present themselves. When people notice these things about you and see that you don't judge them for what they may perceive as negative things about them, they tend to show more of themselves with you, strengthening your relationship in the process. This is the kicker about true acceptance, when you accept people for who they are, they begin to change. It's a natural occurrence and a by-product. We can't go around trying to change by accepting them because then it's not genuine, this only works when it's a true feeling. It's very intriguing to me that when you accept people they change, but as I'm writing this, I see how it all works together. People present themselves in a certain manner for whatever reason they do, some is for protection, some because of trauma, others because of learned behavior; whatever the reason they present is not the point of this. It is that they do present. Acceptance breaks barriers, heals, and creates a level of safety that allows people to come out of their shell and feel safe. I will go deeper into this when I get to the protection part of H.A.R.P. This is why acceptance is so important, it eliminates resistance which is the first step to creating a fight. So many people are at odds with each other because of a lack of acceptance. When I accepted Dontaie for who he was and didn't try to change, annoy, or psychoanalyze him, our relationship changed for the better. Dontaie is my closest male sibling I have. We have been competing at everything for as long as I could remember. Well I was competing with him. I could never beat my brother in anything while growing up, not a race, not basketball, not football, not washing dishes, not dating girls, and the list goes on. I can truly attribute a lot of my competitiveness to him. My older brother Roniae as well, but it's a 6 year difference so there were physical barriers I had to meet first to even try to compete with him. But with Taie, as long as I can remember Dontaie and Neefy were always going at it. Now I no longer compete with my brother, but I enjoy my brother. He's a marathon runner now, I know he hates it when I say that but I'm going to speak it into existence. He actually runs 5k and 2k, but I call it a marathon because it's way too long for me to run. I see what he's doing, and I get pointers that apply to my life, and use them. It's no longer competing. I also notice that in the gym he's no longer opposed to repping heavier weights because he sees it's not going to bulk him up if he continues to do the other things he does as well with the heavy weight. It's great intellectual property to have and it leads us right into our next word.

ACCEPTANCE WORKSHOP

After having read the section above on the acceptance portion of the H.A.R.P concept, take some time to complete the following statements. Make sure that you answer as honestly as you can. The answers are meant to help you to identify areas that you might need to work on and having this workbook section can provide you with good insight.

- Let's be honest, there is something about yourself that you haven't truly accepted, you just don't talk about it. Let's name that thing! When we put a name on it, it takes the air out of it.

- Now that you have said it, repeat it 5 times and feel how much easier it gets to get over it.

- Forgive yourself—As we stated before, the healing process will always begin with forgiveness and many times forgiving ourselves is the hardest step.

Write down all those feelings and thoughts that are coming to your mind and make sure to present them in prayer. Look for the Scriptures that go against them and replace those thoughts with the word of God.

> ## REASSURANCE
>
> **Reassurance**-the action of removing someone's doubts or fears

I've had many battles with this world with my little sister Ashley C. I hated when she would say women need reassurance. I would say reassure yourself, you don't need other words to help you, that's crazy; but boy was I wrong.

I always viewed reassurance as self-doubt, which clearly its' not. I thought when you second guess yourself you needed reassurance to combat the insecurities. Man thank God for growth! Reassurance is so important, and I never knew I needed it and got it until I slowed down to write this book. When I didn't get drafted I tell you this was devastating. I was angry but now knowing anger is a secondary emotion, hindsight tells me I was hurt. For years I carried this hurt. The thought of my wife not believing that the NFL wasn't just a dream, but it was something I actually worked hard enough to obtain bothered me. When my mother in law told me that the dream was over and that now you have a family that you need to take care of, it negatively affected me. I see now that they didn't mean any harm by it. They just wanted what was best

Chapter Eight

for the family from their perspective, so there's no love lost or animosity there at all. Nevertheless, this was my experience and since this is my book, I have to say how I felt. I walked around angry for about five years and when anyone would ever talk to me about the NFL I couldn't comfortably speak because I felt like I missed an opportunity, and I couldn't articulate my thoughts and feelings in the way I'm doing it now. Two things helped me or should I say reassured me and ultimately helped me overcome anger. The first thing was a day in which I was having a random conversation with a complete stranger. I was telling him how I didn't make it to the NFL and how I went to rookie training camp but didn't make the team. He told me that I accomplished more than 99.9 percent of the population by making it that far and to be proud of my accomplishments because truth be told, most people don't even make it to play Division 1 Football. I made it to that plus to rookie training camp, so that's a true honor.

The second was when I got a call from my old coach. It was one random day; I had a cousin who was interested in going to the school that he was at but wasn't on their recruiting list. I called up there and the secretary took it as a routine call. She said there were a lot of kids who were interested in the school, but none of them couldn't make it. I knew that it was standard operations, so I didn't take it personally. When I said my cousin's name, I could feel her face light up through the phone. It was like they had been trying to get in contact with him. She asked me for his Instagram, Facebook, and Twitter handles and at the time he had neither of them. I left my number and was clear to say that he wasn't at my current high school. Well about a week later I got a call from a random unknown number, and I answered. When I got on the phone the coach said "Neefy I've been wanting to talk to you. I messed up with you but now I am able to better connect with these kids I have now." He went on to share a couple more things, but that's all I needed. I was driving home from work, and I had to pull over because I just started crying. It was all the thoughts I had in my mind that I couldn't articulate coming to a head. It felt like releasing the steam of a pressure cooker. I was so relieved when I heard that news and overwhelmed with joy. I see now that it was reassurance, and how important reassurance is. I now see what reassuring a person does internally. It made me whole again and it led to forgiveness. I stopped being mad at him, I stopped blaming him for being the reason I was not going to the NFL, and I also started coaching differently. I never wrote off a player after that and I worked my hardest to connect with all my players on their level.

While I was going through that, I had a very challenging DE at the school I was coaching. He did what other 16-17 year olds did, not give his best, wait until the game to play hard, be late to practices and meetings. He just wasn't used to seeing consequences for his actions. I used to have to bench him for halves at a time. I remember this one particular week, we were playing Okeechobee Brahman Bulls, we were at their school, and I made him dress out, but I didn't play him. I had to show him that his actions were letting his teammates down and that we need him, but we need him to do the right thing when he is supposed to. I remember vividly one of the players came off the field, he was playing both tackle and Defensive end, with

Chapter Eight

his hands on his knees pleading with me to put him in because he was tired, and he couldn't go anymore. At the moment I had to fight back my emotions and stick to my principles because it was hard. After I told him no, I walked off and prayed that God would keep him because the kid was exhausted. The kid really believed he was letting his teammates down. I think that was the straw that broke the camel's back. That was his junior year, after that game I don't recall the kid missing another practice or event. He eventually went on to his senior year and broke the school's record for sacks in a season for sure. We went to an all-American game and was asked in an interview what changed from his Jr. to Sr. season? He went from playing 6 games in his junior year to all 13 games in his senior year. He said, "my coach never let up on me and didn't allow me to give anything other than my best." That was a tearjerker moment for sure, but it never would have happened if I didn't get the reassurance from my coach.

When we listen to others and validate their feelings and thoughts, it creates a space for love. What that looks like in our everyday lives is our parents telling us to be careful of women and we say something like "women?, what makes you think I have all these women?" rather than saying I hear you and understand your concerns and I'm being careful. We understand now our parents aren't trying to control us, it's their way of keeping us safe. When our parents don't have to worry about our well-being, it creates a space for peace. I don't know about you but when my parents are at peace, my life is also peaceful. Let's look at it from a girlfriend's point of view. We know our ladies understand we are beautiful specimens made by God for their enjoyment, and they know other women can see us and like us. We understand groupies are real and present. We can reassure them by letting them know that those groupies aren't our girlfriends and that we chose them because we see ourselves with them. When we give them that, they will definitely get off our backs and stop all the crazy texting or calling all those times when we don't answer the phone when they call. I know we like to say they are crazy and toxic, but by reassuring them we can eliminate all the negative or toxic traits that we don't like about them. That's when she becomes your peace, and as you know, for stress filled workers peace is a true gem. When we have three things, honesty, acceptance, and reassurance, then and only then, will the barriers be broken, and the trust is there for protection to even be a thing.

REASSURANCE WORKSHOP

After having read the section above on the reassurance portion of the H.A.R.P concept, take some time to go through the following statements. Make sure that you answer as honestly as you can. The answers are meant to help you to identify areas that you might need to work on and having this workbook section can provide you with good insight.

1. If you got this far, you are on the right path. I want to let you know you are close to your breakthrough, keep it going, you got this!

   _____

   _____

   _____

2. Reassure your loved one. Write down three things that you are proud of from the person you chose in your honesty entry.

   _____

   _____

   _____

3. Tell that person what you just wrote down. We cannot assume people know what we think about them, telling them directly can be the initial step to a much better relationship.

   _____

   _____

   _____

After having completed step three, write down the person's reaction to what you told them. You will be surprised how healing reassurance can be.

Chapter Eight

PROTECTION

Protect-keep safe from harm or injury

For you to allow someone to protect you, you must trust them. I know a lot of you reading this are asking, how is my girl protecting me? Well this is how women protect us, after reading this you need to give her a hug, buy her some flowers and tell her thank you. Women protect our egos. When we have vulnerable moments with our women or what some consider "pillow talk" and it never comes back up again, that is protection. When you are in a room with people and you are exaggerating the story and that lady doesn't call you out, that is protection. When she knows you don't have any money but wants to be taken out to dinner and she gives you her card so when the waiter hands you the bill you can take out your wallet and feel like a man, although she's paying for it, that's protection. This may be the most important and under viewed way of protection: when a woman keeps your secrets. Not any secrets but those types of secrets like you don't watch scary movies because they make you cry, or that you are truly afraid of water and that's why you don't go to the beach. We need to be honest with ourselves and accept women's ways of protecting us. As macho as we are, it's hard to see protection in a way outside of force, but if we want harmonious friendships with women we must use this.

When you know someone is protecting you, it's like a breath of confidence that you can't let go. You walk with your chest higher and almost feel like you can't be stopped. It's similar to greeting a game plan and you know on 3rd and long in empty they are going to slide their line left, so if you send the 6th one from your left he will come free. You see it on film, you practice it all week and then it comes up at a critical point in the game. The play is called, you know the snap count so you time it perfectly and you come off that edge free. You are aware that the quarterback likes to spin out of pressure, so you anticipate the spin, and he spins right into for a sho'nuff decleater moment. That type of joy that follows is what it feels like to know you are protected.

We also must do some protection. By this I mean to do your best to keep people from hurt or harm. As men, we have the physical compensation, but the emotional aspect of protecting is where we are most vulnerable. To protect emotionally means we allow space for mess ups. We show grace or unmerited favor when people need it the most. We don't emotionally shut people out when they are crying out for help. We must maintain that thought process throughout the entirety of the interaction. This is a daily battle for me. A lot of times I want to show how much I know, but it gets me in trouble because I am more concerned about showing how much I know, rather than getting the desired result. This too gets me sometimes, so when you're reading this don't think that it's all supposed to happen immediately. This too is a journey not a destination so don't be so hard on yourself and allow yourself room to grow.

Chapter Eight

PROTECTION WORKSHOP

After having read the section above on the protection portion of the H.A.R.P concept, take some time to answer the following questions. Make sure that you answer as honestly as you can. The answers are meant to help you to identify areas that you might need to work on and having this workbook section can provide you with good insight.

1. We have established the importance of honesty, with that being said, what do you need protection from?

_____

_____

_____

2. Do you feel comfortable allowing someone to protect you?

_____

_____

_____

3. What techniques are most effective in protecting you?

_____

_____

_____

This is really tough; you have to write down your own protection plan. How do you want to be protected, what are your vulnerabilities and how can you protect yourself with these things present?

Chapter Eight

CHAPTER NINE
MANAGING EMOTIONS

I struggled with putting this content in the book. I was thinking I should save this for my next book, but I would be doing you a disservice. This has to be one of the most important topics that isn't discussed publicly. How do I deal with emotions in a life where I am told it's not ok to be emotional? When I'm playing sports passion is expected, which is an emotion by the way! There is an expectation of me being angry enough to go toe to toe with a 300-pound lineman, 50 snaps a game, but when the lights are off, I need to somehow shut off and not be emotional. This is the single most important reason in my opinion for athletes, especially football, but across all sports that need someone to shed some light on this. Teams now have sports psychologists on the sidelines because they understand the stress and pressure athletes are put under, but it seems not to transfer to life outside of sports. My goal in this chapter is to show you how to harness, take authority over, control and master your emotions.

> **HARNESS- CONTROL AND MAKE USE OF**

When we harness our emotions, we must gather them up for our benefit. Emotions are indicators of different things. If you like something, your body will send your brain positive emotions and will want you to continue to do what you were doing in order to get that. When you don't like something, negative emotions tend to come up. I later learned nothing is negative or positive but it's what you make of it. There are the same number of electrons, negatively charged particles, as protons, positively charged particles in everything, we must choose which one we want to focus on.

When we harness these emotions, we are gathering them to use them for our benefit. I know that all things work for me, nothing happens to me, but rather everything happens for me. My bible tells me that in Romans 8:28. So in any situation that arises, I lean on that heavily. Most recently, I took a coaching job about 400 miles away from my family to make ends meet. My wife is back in school becoming a Nurse Assistant and she could no longer work. I have been a teacher my whole adult life and she was a DNP. This was a major obstacle we had to overcome. Her leaving a 6-figure salary to go back to school with a recession looming was crazy to me, but it was bold and took faith to do. I know that you can't please God without faith, from reading Hebrews 11:6. I didn't know what to do, my $50k salary wasn't enough to maintain our lifestyle while she wasn't working. However, I prayed and fasted, then randomly I received a call from a coach I used to work with. He asked me if I was willing to take a job in South Georgia. Things worked out, the salary was enough, and we made it work. We had a great season and an even more promising basketball season. We won 6 games my first season compared to the previous 3 seasons which had won a total of 2. Everything was going well until I got called to the principal's office and they told me my contract wasn't being renewed after my first year. At first, I was devastated, angry, and was seeking blood. I wanted revenge because I felt tried, used, and abused. After two weeks of going back and forth and hearing compelling arguments on both sides, I decided that I was going to trust God. He brought me here for a reason and he's always had something better for me after leaving a place. I was reminded that when we operate outside of God's will for us we tend to bring on things we didn't want to. I had to get back to the dwelling place of the Most High like in Psalms 91. This is when I was reminded that I've had worse things happen and that God has always had me. I had to change my attitude about what was going on, the only two things that I can control are my attitude and my actions. God has everything else. I was reminded of how Joseph was sold into slavery, and he didn't get upset with his brothers. His mindset was whoever buys, we will be blessed because I am blessed, and that's what happened. He got up to Potiphar's house and had access to everything but his wife. She gave him access to her, but he refused it and got sent to prison because she said he tried to sexually assault her. When he was in jail for that he interpreted a dream for one of Pharaoh's people. That turned out to be a major turning point in his life because Pharaoh put in in control of the grain and he saved Egypt, along with his family. He never wavered on his stance in any obstacle that he faced. That same God that he had is the same God that's in us. I know that no matter the situation, I am God's, and he will take care of me. He's never left me or failed me, and this too means he has something greater for me. This next step is very important, we have harnessed our emotions and now we have to control them.

> **Control- determine the behavior or supervise the running of, we must use these things called emotions for our benefit.**

We have authority over our emotions, and we must mention our stance in the face of whatever obstacle we are facing. I have made a decree in my life that God is better than the best thing that the world has to offer. This has allowed me to stay and stand tall in any situation I have going on. My faith allows me to be in places that I would have never even dreamed about going to. My faith also allows me to control my emotions. When I heard my wife talk about the liquid she saw in my son's head, my emotions went everywhere. I was hurt, sad, and distraught. There was nothing easy about that situation for me and when you read it, if it made it seem that way, I would like to apologize. That was one of the hardest things I've ever done. I prayed for a son, and God gave me a son. I used to say she was going to get pregnant with twin boys, and Gavyn and Enzo would have been their names. I used to say this every day to anyone in ear shot. I was dedicated and sold on this situation. So to hear I got a son, but it wasn't what I prayed for, brought me exactly to a story I read in a book. The story goes that there was a drought in the land for 3 years. Crops were dying, people were hurting, and everyone needed water. A rabbi went out in the field and drew a circle and decided that he wasn't going to leave the circle until his prayers were answered. He began praying and a downpour came, the rain was hard enough to cause flash floods. He told God that this was not what he was praying for, so he stayed there. Then, all of a sudden the rain lightened up to a soft refreshing mist, but he said that's not what he prayed for either. He stayed praying until the perfect rain came down, when it did, he said thank you and got up. He didn't just accept anything, he waited until God did exactly what he wanted. That's when I told my wife we didn't get a son for this, we didn't wait all these years to have a son for this. I thought about Abrahm having to sacrifice Isaac and with perfect timing the ram appeared in the bushes because of his obedience. I knew it was time sensitive and I always wanted to be a friend of God's, like Abraham, Moses, and David, so I went into action. That's when I made my declaration to God and reminded my wife that God didn't bring us here to leave us here. This was a crucial part because had I given in to the emotions, we wouldn't be here today. My son's name is Gavyn Enzo Moffett or gem for short because he's so precious to me. This is what controlling emotions looks like, it's tough but necessary for the betterment of not only myself but everything connected to me.

Having authority over your emotions is a key, we know we control them and harness them, but they could be like a dog with a leash on that continues to pull you. When training dogs, one must show who has the authority or like I like to say the top dog. When you have a dog that's a puller, every time they pull I stop. I show them I won't allow tugging of the leash and if they can't walk without tugging, they won't walk. This is how we have to take authority over our emotions.

> **Authority—the power or right to give orders, make decisions, and enforce obedience**

To do this we must understand that the spectrum of our emotions are one. This foundational principles that I'm about to give will be explained to you like they were explained to me.

1. Exposure determines how we think
2. What you think determines how we feel
3. Feeling impact our decisions
4. Our decisions determine our actions.
5. Our actions create our habits
6. Habits create our character
7. Character determines our destination

Once this is understood, I will show you how to take authority over your emotions. Emotions are tied to feelings; feelings come from what we think, so when we change our thinking, our feelings have to change. This is why the bible says *"Finally, brothers and sisters, whatever is true, whatever is noble, whatever is right, whatever is pure, whatever is lovely, whatever is admirable—if anything is excellent or praiseworthy—think about such things."* (Phil 4:8). Our thoughts determine everything and if you are struggling with your thoughts, you must change what you are exposed to and listen to. Faith comes by hearing states another bible verse, so in order to believe something you must hear it and make a conscious decision to believe it. This is why affirmations work, why we read books, and why we hear lectures. We get exposed to things that will change our beliefs and trajectory. I didn't even think of writing a book. I used to write down my thoughts and I was even a creative writing major in college briefly, but the thought about writing a book came from my brother Geno. He said, *"Man we should write a book, the wealth of knowledge we have should be put to use."* It took him to die for me to make the decision to write, but I know the more I write, the closer I am to him. It all works out no matter how you cut it. Expose yourself to different things along your journey so that you can change your feelings about anything. I had to learn to use my authority for my benefit. I was always told I was controlling in relationships to the point where anytime the word control is used, I would just leave the conversation. I wouldn't do anything that could be considered controlling. That got me nowhere! I had to realize that I have wisdom, power, and a sound mind and I can use that for my good. Controlling never bothered me ever again. I actually now openly tell people that I am controlling, the difference now is that I can control myself. I never try to control other people. I had to learn that when you are trying to control other people, you don't have control over yourself. This is a great lesson that I had to learn. This is how I can stand boldly now and say I have authority over my emotions. This was hard but impactful, very much like matt drills. The pre-spring training that we did at FSU that everyone hated. I think in my career I did the most matt drills ever and I HATED them with passion. I went back every time except one. I got 0's in something every time. I even got a temporary cast just to do matt drills. I wasn't allowed to be in the track team, which in my tenure won 3 national championships because of matt drill. If I had known what I know today, my approach would have been way different, and I probably wouldn't be writing this book. I would be on a yacht with beautiful women dancing like Ciara on her video. This gives me an opportunity to reach 1000's of young people though because of my stance on this, God's ways are always better than what I could ever imagine. And now I can be on a yacht with my family enjoying a nice vacation.

> **Mastery- comprehensive knowledge or skill in a subject or accomplishment or control or superiority over someone or something**

This is an ongoing process that you have to continue to recreate one situation after another. This is the work that goes along, and we will dig deeper into this at the end of the chapter.

Whatever you think of something, that's what it is. Simply put, I determine the value of things by what I think of it. So as I think of myself, that is what is. Point blank, period! Nothing else has that type of power except humans. You have immeasurable power within you that you can tap into. Your life will be exactly like you see it to be once you understand this. With that said, my feelings are a mirror image of what I think of myself. I have had a lot of things guard my thoughts and ultimately affect my feelings. Things that before this I wouldn't admit. Feelings of not enough, being the younger brother and having to fight for everything I got. Thoughts of not being like my daddy, thoughts of letting my family down when I didn't go to the league. Thoughts that I wasn't good enough to go to the league, then trying to convince myself and people that I was more than capable. Fear of the unknown being expressed as anger. Suicidal thoughts, sadness and many more have been things that blocked my feelings. Understanding now that where my attention goes, my energy flows. My thoughts have been transformed and I can now be in the space to share the growth in my feelings. We can break the societal norms that we have constructed and build exactly what we want to build. Let's break these chains while we are on the subject.

> **"Men have less emotions than women"**

This is a lie from the pit of hell and Satan can no longer brainwash us into thinking this. It is said to be a fact that women display more emotions than men. When it comes to emotions, men are the warehouse and women are the store front. They show them and display them, we house them within and are never to be seen. We have to acknowledge that they are there in order to move forward in what we are doing.

> **"Men internalize their emotions"**

Men display their emotions; it's just almost always shown as anger. Anger is the only emotion we display, and it covers all other emotions, but in therapy I've learned that anger is a secondary emotion. When we dive deeper and identify why we are angry, we will see exactly what is leading the anger and it is emotions.

> **"Men grunt as instead of verbally expressing"**

Think of an angry grandpa. He doesn't say anything, he just moans, and grandma knows exactly what that means. That is something that needs to be changed, men have voices as well and if truth be told, we can use our voices for way more than things that strike our ego. We are fully capable of expressing ourselves without violence to get a task complete. We often choose not to, but we have to remember that it's a choice we can make something different.

I was so afraid of losing control and everything I thought I had built for myself by expressing emotions, that I shut them off. They are now reflecting on my weight. As I'm writing this, I am coming off being the heaviest I've ever been in my life. An internalization approach has got me way overweight just holding on to everything because I had a misunderstanding of emotions. I'm thinking it makes me a man by not showing any emotions however, the reality of the situation is that by not acknowledging emotions it has led me to more pain and hurt. If I had just acknowledged them in the beginning a lot of things could have been prevented. God has not given me the spirit of fear, but he has given me wisdom, power, and a sound mind. Fear no longer resides in me, and when it comes up, I know that perfect love casts out all fear. This journey of totally depending on God is scary but not fearful. Truth be told the only part that scares me is the validation of others, especially what my wife and kids think of me. I had to shake that and really ask myself, am I going to please God or my wife? In pleasing God, I know my wife will be pleased because he gave her to me. Pleasing my wife doesn't mean I'm pleasing God though, so I have to be mindful and stay focused on depending on God. Pleasing God means operating out of faith, using my spirit to connect and communicate with God. I trust and know that my body is a temple (dwelling place of God) so God is in me, and I become him, and he becomes me. I wasn't being true to the God in me by seeking outside validation. When I move in sincerity and love that's all the validation I need. I can't afford to give that away anymore because it will KILL ME, literally. Identifying these emotions and expressing my feelings have moved me to this place of peace and has released a huge burden that I had put on myself.

REFLECTION:

1. If we are being completely honest with ourselves, do you think you are led more by fear or love?

___

___

___

2. If you answer the previous question how you intended, skip this one. If you didn't, how can you incorporate more of the emotion that you want into your everyday living?

___

___

___

3. Write about all the things you don't like about you emotionally to get it out, we need to make room for new experiences by letting go of the old.

EPILOGUE

After reading this, take these principles not as something that you have to do, but as a reference and example to guide you through your life. Take the ones that apply and use them for you. Make sure that you are free from the mental bondage of the "in the box" thinking and live life on your own terms.

> *Many of us just ride the wave because we are unaware that we can control the ocean.*

www.ingramcontent.com/pod-product-compliance
Lightning Source LLC
Chambersburg PA
CBHW071402080526
44587CB00017B/3157